duck flowing mountain salmon
autumn drizzle marshm chen
snowflakes kitten food wooden moon
petals geese happy dogs pumpkins evening
baseball calm puppy trees happy doll
skirt branch bamboos sneaker flowers
frog pond water happy pumpkins starlight
grandfather puppy bamboos pumpkin
sailboat branch frog oceanside dewdrops
homework water skirt sailboat dogs rain
dancing trees mountain laughter mom
dogs flowing autumn duck salmon puppy
autumn drizzle marshmallows kitchen rose
snowflakes kitten food wooden on lights
flowers geese happy rain pumpkins

Haiku

asian arts & crafts for creative kids

Patricia Donegan

TUTTLE PUBLISHING

Boston • Rutland, Vermont • Tokyo

Every attempt has been made to contact the authors, artists, or copyright holders of the works included in this book. Our apologies to anyone who was overlooked—please contact us to ensure that we give proper credit in future editions.

"and now the cat comes" from *Blush of Winter Moon* by Patricia Machmiller (Jacarana Press, 2001). Reprinted with permission of the author.

"Serenade" by Garry Gay and John Thompson from *Frogpond* magazine, 1998, xxi:1. Reprinted with permission of the authors.

"Tundra" by Cor van den Heuvel and "an empty elevator" by Jack Cain from *The Haiku Anthology: English Language Haiku by Contemporary American and Canadian Poets*, Cor van den Heuvel, ed. (Anchor Books, 1974). Reprinted with permission of the authors.

"bright sun" by Jim Kacian and "quiet evening" by Anita Virgil from *The Haiku Anthology: Haiku and Senryu in English*, Cor van den Heuvel, ed. (W.W. Norton & Co., 1999). Reprinted with permission of the authors.

All children's haiku and illustrations from *Haiku by Children* (anthologies from "The World's Children's Haiku Contests") © 1990, 1995, 1997 and 1999 by the JAL Foundation of Tokyo. Reprinted with permission of the JAL Foundation.

"in the rain" by John Brandi; "sudden shower" by Margaret Chula; "all night" by Penny Harter; "Holding the water" by William J. Higginson; "spring chill" by Bruce Ross; "summer storm" by David Sutter; "Letting" by vincent tripi; "Lily" by Nicolas Virgilio; "piano practice" by Raymond Roseliep; "After the rain" by George Swede; "soaking up" by Alexis Rotella; "beyond the sink" by Marlene Mountain from *Haiku Moment*, Bruce Ross, ed. © 1993 by Bruce Ross. Reprinted with permission of Tuttle Publishing:

"pausing" from *in this blaze of sun* by Elizabeth Searle Lamb (From Here Press, 1975). Reprinted with permission of the author.

"at its bottom" from *Kiyoko's Sky: The Haiku of Kiyoko Tokutomi*, Patricia Machmiller and Fay Aoyagi, trans. (Brooks Books, 2002). Reprinted with permission of the publisher.

"sunlight is shining" from *Kyoto Dwelling* by Edith Shiffert. © 1987 by Edith Shiffert. Reprinted with permission of Tuttle Publishing.

"cinnamon wafts", "Valentine Chocolate" and "one more birthday gift" unpublished by Kris Kondo and her class. Reprinted with permission of the author.

"one by one" unpublished by Sato Kazuo. Reprinted with permission of the author.

Library of Congress Cataloging-in-Publication Data

Donegan, Patricia
    Haiku : Asian arts & crafts for creative kids / Patricia Donegan
        p. cm
    Summary: Introduces the form of Japanese poetry known as haiku, explores the seven keys to writing haiku, and provides instructions for five haiku projects, including creating haiga, or illustrated haiku.
    Includes bibliographical references and index.
    ISBN 0-8048-3501-2 (hc.)
    1. Creative writing (Elementary education)—Juvenile literature. 2. Haiku—Study and teaching (Elementary)—Activity programs—Juvenile literature. 3. English language—Composition exercises—Study and teaching (Elementary)—Activity programs—Juvenile literature. [1. Creative writing. 2. Haiku. 3. English language—Composition and exercises.] I. Title

LB1576.D628 2003
372.62'3—dc21   2003054095

Distributed by

North America, Latin America, and Europe
Tuttle Publishing
Distribution Center
Airport Industrial Park
364 Innovation Drive
North Clarendon, VT 05759-9436
Tel: (802) 773-8930
Fax: (802) 773-6993
Email: info@tuttlepublishing.com

Japan
Tuttle Publishing
Yaekari Building, 3F
5-4-12 Osaki, Shinagawa-ku
Tokyo 141-0032
Tel: (03) 5437-0171
Fax: (03) 5437-0755
Email: tuttle-sales@gol.com

Asia Pacific
Berkeley Books Pte. Ltd.
130 Joo Seng Road
#06-01/03 Olivine Building
Singapore 368357
Tel: (65) 6280-3320
Fax: (65) 6280-6290
Email: inquiries@periplus.com.sg

First edition
09 08 07 06 05 04 03   9 8 7 6 5 4 3 2 1
Printed in Singapore
Illustrations by Masturzh Jeffrey

contents

Dedicated to
all the world's children who have the "haiku eyes"
to bring about a more peaceful world

Acknowledgments

Thanks to Kazuo Sato, mentor and haiku master, for his suggestions on teaching haiku to children; to the JAL Foundation, especially Shunichi Shibohta and Ritsuko Kamata, for enthusiastically giving permission for use of materials on haiku and haiga from *JAL Children's Haiku Contest Anthologies*; to Tadashi Kondo, for his advice and vision about *renku*; to Kris Young Kondo, for her materials for the renga chapter; to Eiko Yachimoto, for renku information about the *shisan* form; to late haiku master Seishi Yamaguchi, who taught me the importance of the *kigo* (season word); to the Fulbright Foundation, for a research grant to do the co-translation with Yoshie Ishibashi for the book *Chiyo-ni: Woman Haiku Master,* and thus learn about haiku more deeply; to meditation masters, for showing me the haiku moment; to Yoshie Ishibashi, for translation work and heart support; to my parents, Janet and Daniel Donegan, for encouragement and book suggestions; to Charles Trumbull, for haiku resource information; and to acquisitions editor Jennifer Lantagne, for asking me to do this project.

As kids, you already have "haiku eyes"—a way to see the world openly and freshly. Matsuo Basho (1644–1694), the most famous haiku poet, said that to write haiku you need to have the eyes and heart of a child. This book's purpose is to show you the way to write haiku, to teach you to take your "haiku eyes" and put what you see and feel down on paper. It is an introduction to haiku, a unique part of the culture and arts of Japan.

You can use this book by yourself, or with your friends, your brother or sister, your parents, or even your teacher. You can write haiku by yourself or with others. You can use it any way you want. This book takes you through steps and explains what seeing the world with haiku eyes means. It explains what haiku is and is not; it gives you the seven keys to guide you to write haiku; it tells the importance of the seasons and nature in writing haiku; and it guides you to write what you see. It also covers other haiku activities, such as haiku with stories (*haibun*), haiku with drawings (*haiga*), and grouplike haiku with friends (*renga*).

For Adults

Although this book is aimed at children, it can also be used by teenagers and adults—people of any age who are either beginners at haiku or needing to refresh their understanding. This simple and clear approach is an introduction to this amazingly small practice from Japanese culture, which can truly enrich our lives. Haiku can help kids and adults alike to connect to the world of nature and people—to see the deep interconnectedness of our small world, perhaps even making a step toward peace.

This book is meant to guide children to create haiku on their own or with friends; however, the best way for children to learn is to practice with a parent, teacher, older child, or adult. It is important that we share with the children in our lives this way of looking at the world and recording haiku moments. Haiku may help us all to slow down, relax, and stop and see what is around us, so that we can appreciate our world and everyday life more.

So when children learn haiku, they are learning more than just poetry. They learn a fresh and sensitive way to see and connect to nature and the world—and usually become happier and more respectful. They also sharpen their skills in observing things around them. Children strengthen their language skills by learning to express their feelings and ideas more clearly in words and they also expand their creativity, just through this tiny form known as haiku. Best of all, they can always enjoy writing haiku!

preface

old pond—
frog jumps in
sound of the water

— Matsuo Basho (Japanese poet, 1644–1694)

These three short lines make up a haiku, which is also one of the world's most famous poems. It is simple: it tells something about nature and about one little moment in time taken from real experience. Haiku are always there, waiting to be noticed, waiting for us to stop and look and listen to what is happening around us.

Haiku is the world's shortest poetry, but also the most popular form of poetry today. In fact, it is now so popular all over the world that some people don't know that it originated in Japan. Haiku became popular in Japanese culture over three hundred years ago and has now spread all over the world, even to you. Haiku isn't "fancy" poetry, but poetry for everyone. All kinds of people write haiku: Long ago in Japan, the samurai, geisha, shopkeepers, and farmers wrote haiku, and today anyone from schoolchildren to senior citizens write haiku as well. In fact, in Japan, haiku is still a part of everyday life: daily newspapers print haiku; Itoen prints haiku on its cans of green tea drinks; and almost every school and town has a haiku group or club that publishes its own haiku magazine. But anyone, not just people from Japan, can enjoy haiku.

What is it about haiku that people like? One thing is its simplicity—that is, simple noticing. Haiku is simply noticing, noting and recording moments that are happening around us all the time—moments that make us wake up and see and appreciate the world around us more. This moment could be something beautiful, such as a fresh breeze against one's face on a hot summer day, the first snowfall on the car windshield, the smell of the earth after a rainstorm. Or sometimes it could be a sad or bad thing, like a dead bird lying in the sidewalk, a fight with a friend, a homeless woman sleeping in the bus station. It could be something happening in the same space in which we breathe, or it could be an image we see in a movie on television or on the Internet, such as blue planet Earth floating in space, a starving child in a faraway land, people rescued after an earthquake, the planting of tree seedlings to protect the forests. As you can see, anything can be the subject of haiku, because haiku are happening around us all the time.

Capturing these little haiku moments in words is what makes a haiku, and that creation depends on how open our eyes are to the world around us. It is a matter of seeing with clear and open eyes what is in front of our noses right now. You can look up and see the big things, as in this haiku:

> **wild sea—**
> **lying over Sado island**
> **the galaxy**
>
> —Basho

Or you can look down to see the small things, as in this haiku:

> **butterfly—**
> **what's it dreaming**
> **fanning its wings?**
>
> —Chiyo-ni (or Kaga no Chiyo, Japanese poet, 1703–1775)

Often it is through the small things that we learn about the big things. The main point of haiku is to connect to things around us, especially nature, with an open eye and open heart—that is, seeing the world freshly, with "haiku eyes."

Another reason that people like haiku is its simple writing. Of course, we can just enjoy what we see, and not write our observations down; but if we wish to note them and record them and share them with others, it is fairly easy, if we practice. First we must practice seeing, and then practice expressing the seeing in words. But in order to do that, we need some guidelines to follow. Here is a list of seven simple things to understand that will help you to write haiku.

Once understood and practiced, these qualities will naturally become a part of your haiku writing without thinking about them. Let me briefly explain these guidelines.

the seven keys to writing haiku

The Seven Keys to Writing Haiku

Use these seven keys as your checklist when you begin writing your own haiku.

1. Form: Your haiku should have three lines with or without a seventeen syllable count. It should be one breath long.

2. Image (a picture or sketch): Your haiku should have a descriptive image—for example, not "a flower," but instead "a purple iris in the sun."

3. Kigo (Season Word): Your haiku should refer to nature and hint at the day's season or weather.

4. Here and Now: You should write from real experience or memory, not imagination; record the present moment.

5. Feeling: Your haiku should not explain or tell, but instead show the feeling through your image.

6. Surprise: Your haiku should have an "ah!" moment that wakes us up.

7. Compassion: Your haiku should express openheartedness toward nature.

Key 1: Form

in English (three lines)

> old pond—
> frog jumps in
> sound of the water

in Japanese (seventeen syllables)

> furuike ya (five syllables)
> kawazu tobikomu (seven syllables)
> mizu no oto (five syllables)

If you look in the dictionary you will find that haiku is defined as a short Japanese poem, usually about nature, having a seventeen-syllable count. As in the frog haiku above, all traditional Japanese haiku had three parts with a five-, seven-, five-syllable count, making seventeen syllables in all. These haiku were usually written in one line, using black ink and a calligraphy brush. Today most Japanese still write haiku in one long vertical line down the page. You may have heard that, in English, haiku is like a syllable counting game, but that is not the important thing for haiku in English. Haiku is an experience, not an act of counting syllables. The important thing is experiencing the "haiku moment" and connecting with nature.

In English, it is best to write haiku in three lines, with no specific syllable count. In fact, haiku should only be as long as one breath. In English, that would equal about eight words per haiku,

which is equal to a Japanese haiku. In Japanese, seventeen syllables makes about six words, but seventeen syllables in English usually makes about twelve words or more, because the languages are very different. So, in English, seventeen syllables, in most cases, would be too long for haiku. Try to stick to one breath of about six to ten words for your haiku. To test this, read your haiku aloud to see if it fits into one breath. Why do this? Well, haiku is the experience of capturing the moment—and the moment disappears quickly, like the moment of hearing the splash of the frog jumping into the water. That one moment is like a surprise, when we say "ahhh!" or "oooh!," which is also very short. The surprise takes our breath away. That is the "haiku moment," which lasts only for one short breath, and so the haiku must be short to recapture that moment.

Of course, just for fun, you may want to try to write some haiku by counting the syllables of the words: the first line has five syllables, the second line has seven, and the third line has five. As in this example, some rare poets can write good haiku using the seventeen syllable count in English:

> (5) . . . and now the cat comes
> (7) in the moonlight his shadow
> (5) darker than himself

—Patricia Machmiller (American poet, 1941–)

But you might find that the seventeen syllables may make your haiku sound too long and awkward, like it does in most haiku and in this version of the same frog haiku:

there is an old pond (five syllables)
the frog is jumping in it (seven syllables)
sound of the water (five syllables)

So I recommend the best way is *not* to use seventeen syllables, but instead just three lines. To make the three lines of the English balanced, it is good to try and make the second line longer than the other lines. Make the haiku short, one breath long. Pay attention to the "ah!" moment in nature, say your haiku aloud to make sure it is one breath long, and pay attention to the sound of your words—your haiku should sound smooth and natural and have rhythm like your own way of talking. Practice listening while reading your haiku aloud—train your ears, as well as your eyes, for haiku.

Another thing to remember is that haiku is not a sentence, so it does not begin with a capital letter and end with a period. Look at the Basho frog poem again. This haiku has no capital or period, but it does have a dash mark. Sometimes a dash, colon, comma, or exclamation point is used to show a break in the haiku. This break is called a "cutting word" (*kireji* in Japanese). In Japanese, the break is shown by little words like *ya, keri,* or *kana*. This break is important, and is usually after the first or second line. You can see in the frog haiku that the dash used at the end of the first line, after the word *pond*, is used to show the break; in

Japanese, *furuike* means "pond," and *ya* is the pause word. This pause will help to create a stronger feeling in your haiku, so be aware of this when you want to tell your haiku moment. Just keep practicing step by step.

Key 2: Image

Haiku gives a picture or makes a sketch of a scene, like a snapshot from a camera. It is important to use good images to do this. In haiku, the image is simply a word or group of words that present something relating to the senses—something that can be seen, heard, touched, smelled, or tasted—especially images from nature. Usually a haiku uses one or two images. This frog haiku is good because it has sharp nature images and we can see the scene clearly: the pond, the frog, and the splash of water. It is easier to create a strong image when you are more descriptive. For example, try not to use a general word like *flower*, but instead tell what kind of flower it is, like *purple iris*. To make an even stronger image, you can put the flower in a scene, like "a purple iris in the sun" or "a purple iris in the sun of my grandmother's backyard." This makes a strong picture for your haiku.

It is important to use strong images from nature as in these haiku:

rain drops fall
wet and cool
leaves spread full

—Uriah Muhammad (age seven, United States)

a spiderweb
a thread of silver
woven by the wind

—Carlos tun Ruiz (age eleven, Mexico)

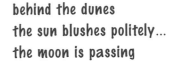

In these haiku we can see and feel the raindrops and the leaves, the silver spider web and the wind. The key idea is not to tell or explain to the reader what you saw, but just to show what you saw through the image. For example, if you look up at the moon at night, do not say, "I looked up and saw the beautiful moon," but rather describe the scene you saw, as in this haiku:

the full moon conjures
a silvery street
in my room

—Franziska Stagneth (age ten, Germany)

Here the poet is letting the image speak for itself to show the beautiful moon. To write a good haiku, one must see the world clearly and write it down clearly, using good images. And since haiku is so short, the reader must be able to experience, in three short lines, the "seeing" that stopped the poet and made him or her write the haiku. Here are some other haiku about the moon:

behind the dunes
the sun blushes politely...
the moon is passing

—Zeina Chamas (age twelve, Saudia Arabia)

the leaves
are lit by the pale
moonlight

—Paul Shin (age nine, United States)

Here are some other hints about using images. Try to not use the words *like* or *as* in a comparison, such as "winter branches *like* icy fingers," because it weakens the image. Also try not to repeat the same type of words, like *bright* and *sunny* because they express the same idea and do not add to your haiku. Try not to use words like *sad* or *beautiful* either, because these words explain—they don't show. Here are some examples of haiku that use sharp images:

in the evening twilight
only the mushrooms
are illuminated

—Keiji Beta (age twelve, Japan)

evening breeze—
water splashes against
a blue heron's legs

—Yosa Buson (Japanese poet, 1716–1783)

Usually you should use one main image. One way to make this image more interesting is to connect it to something else. It is important to show the spark between the images—that moment of surprise that made you stop and look more and say, "Ah! now I see ..." It is the spark between the two images of the "twilight" and "the mushrooms" or "the breeze" and the "blue heron" that makes a haiku interesting. This spark is sometimes shown by a break or pause, as in the frog or heron haiku.

Key 3: Kigo (Season Word)

off they leap
grasshopper mother and child
and turn to grass

—Katsushi Hosokawa (age ten, Japan)

Basho said, "Follow nature and return to nature." Haiku is a way for us to reconnect to nature, because it makes us aware of our relationship to nature and the environment. A "season word" is a word referring to the present day's weather and the season, such as spring, summer, autumn, or winter. How many and what kinds of seasons you have depend on where you live in the world. In Japan, which has four seasons, the custom became to include a word referring to the seasons in the haiku. This season word was called the *kigo*. From the eighth to twelfth centuries, when Japanese

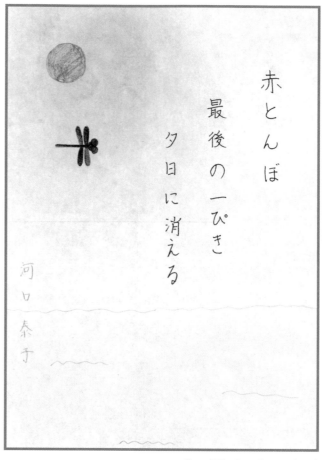

Katsushi Hosokawa (age ten, Japan)

people got together for parties or court poetry contests, a season theme was used to start the poem, such as "snow" or "moon." As haiku developed from the sixteenth century on, specific season words were used, such as *cherry blossom* for spring, *seashell* for summer, *cricket* for autumn, and *north wind* for winter. Of course, these season words are closely connected to the weather, season, and lifestyles of Japan, which may be different from other countries of the world. So you must find your own season words by observing the weather and the seasonal changes of your own land. Sometimes you can even use the name of the season, like *winter* or *spring*, instead of a descriptive word, as in these haiku:

> **at its bottom**
> **all things are visible**
> **winter river**
>
> —Kiyoko Tokutomi (Japanese poet, 1928–2002)

> **in the spring rain**
> **bamboo grass shows its face**
> **pandas get happy**
>
> —Guo Chong Yu (age twelve, China)

But why even use a season word? Using a season word in a haiku encourages the poet to connect to the natural world around her or him, and relate to this moment, this time, this place. And using the season word makes the haiku deeper and more universal. The most important thing to remember is what Basho said about nature. He talked about the importance of feeling close to nature, and he said about writing haiku, "Learn about the pine from the pine and learn about the bamboo from the bamboo."

In the frog poem, there are several words relating to nature: the pond, the frog, and the water itself. For the Japanese, the season word is *frog*, which is

known to be in the season of spring. Knowing this *one* word helps the reader to imagine all the things connected to the spring season and the feeling it brings to our hearts. That is one reason haiku can say much in only a few words. The season word acts like a code. Most poets use a season word, but some poets write "no-season-word haiku," using instead a nature word that could indicate any season, like *mountain* or *forest,* as in this haiku:

> **returning from the mountain**
> **father's clothes**
> **smell of the forest**
>
> —Akira Taniguchi (age twelve, Japan)

Or this haiku where the nature images, of moss, tree, and swamp could be in any season:

> **moss so green**
> **grows on the tree trunk**
> **in the dark damp swamp**
>
> —Karen Stone (age eight, United States)

And some modern poets do not use any nature or season word at all, as in this famous haiku:

> **an empty elevator**
> **opens**
> **closes**
>
> —Jack Cain (Canadian haiku poet, 1940–)

Although it is an interesting poem, it is not really a haiku in the traditional sense, because it does not have any reference to nature. So I would recommend that you stick to using some kind of nature image or season word to keep the spirit of haiku.

A big reason for using a nature or season word is that it makes us less centered on ourselves and more centered on others and on nature. And remember that nature includes the human world, so you can also write a haiku mixing nature and our human world, as shown in these haiku:

> a strong wind blew
> the roof right off my house
> that night I counted stars

—Aree La-ongthong (age eleven, Thailand)

> small green growing things
> in my old dirty locker
> on my ham sandwich

—Ashley (age twelve, Canada)

Key 4: Here and Now

Haiku is a way to slow down in our modern, speedy world. When we slow down, we are able to catch the moment of haiku, and then we can relax and appreciate things more. Basho's idea in a nutshell is that haiku is what is happening in this moment, this time, this place. The best haiku are usually written from our real experience in the moment—that is, in the here and now. Sometimes we write from the memory of our real experience, which is fine. And some people even write haiku from their imagination, which is called "desk haiku." But the best haiku come from real experience. If you have an open mind, "haiku eyes," and can slow down for a moment, you can catch the haiku all around you. The story behind the frog poem is a good example of a haiku coming from the poet's real experience. One day, Basho was sitting with his friends in a quiet tea garden. He and his friends would talk a bit, and then relax and be quiet, to listen to nature. Then, within the silence, suddenly he heard the sound of a frog leaping into the water of the nearby pond. Basho was happily surprised and immediately wrote down this haiku with the help of his friends. As you can see, haiku is simply appreciating what is already around us. See and discover what is here, as in this haiku:

> for a second a butterfly
> settles on my cheek
> I must not breathe

—Myriam Suchet (age fifteen, France)

> the electric bulb is shining
> flies are sitting on it
> enjoying it

—Anastasiya Blank (age eleven, USSR)

along with spring leaves
my child's teeth
are coming in

—Nakamura Kusatao (Japanese poet, 1901–1983)

Key 5: Feeling

Haiku are usually known to be little sketches of nature, but a good haiku usually moves the reader's feeling in some way. It can be a big emotion, like sadness, or a subtle feeling about something beautiful or funny. Yet the feeling is not said directly. It is never explained, but instead shown through the image in the haiku. We would not write, "It is lonely," but would show the feeling through an image. For example, we would not write, "the lonely frog" or "the frog looks lonely," but rather describe the frog so that it seems lonely, as in "a tiny frog sits in the cold rain." This creates a lonely picture. In Basho's frog poem, the feeling is not of loneliness, but instead a feeling of quietness and relaxation, with a sense of surprise. Here are some examples of letting the image express the feeling:

loneliness

sitting on the beach
a hermit crab
stuck in a bottle

—Christopher Andrews (age twelve, Australia)

sadness

watching the sunset
sitting on a grassy cliff
after father's death

—Ainslie Collness (age twelve, Australia)

wonder

sitting low on the grass
red bug crawls across my hand—
his whole world

—Nancy Perez (age ten, United States)

Key 6: Surprise

To write a haiku, we must be awake to our world. When our mind is here, and not asleep or crowded by thoughts, we can see more clearly. Sometimes we are surprised by this discovery, although it was there all the time. This "clear seeing" itself becomes the surprise or fresh moment. This in turn makes us appreciate everyday life more. For example, as in Basho's frog haiku, the last line is the sound of surprise breaking the silence. Haiku is the experience of catching the moment— catching the moment of hearing the splash of the frog jumping into the water before it is gone. The surprise takes our breath away and we say "ahhh!" That is the surprise that makes a haiku moment. It lasts only for one breath, so the haiku is short, to recapture that one little moment.

> **hit by**
> **a raindrop—**
> **the snail closes up**
>
> —Yosa Buson

Also, we don't try to surprise or shock on purpose, but instead we just sit still and notice what is here, like "the sunlight on our plate at breakfast." For if we see what is here and write about what is here, the haiku will take care of itself. Of course we have to practice the form of haiku to do this.

Humor also comes out of surprise—that is, noticing the strange or funny things in this world is also a part of haiku seeing. Seeing the world through haiku eyes is always a surprise in some way, as in these haiku:

> **the night comes**
> **stars shining brightly**
> **tough luck Mr. Burglar!**
>
> —Elizabeth Wairimu (age nine, Kenya)

> **the warbler**
> **poops**
> **on a slender plum branch**
>
> —Uejima Onitsura (Japanese poet, 1661–1738)

Humor is a big part of haiku. But there is also a cousin of haiku known as *senryu*.

A senryu does not have to be about nature, but it does have to express something funny usually about people and our world. Sometimes it is hard to tell the difference between senyru and haiku.

Here are two senryu by unknown Japanese poets from the eighteenth century:

> **in a mouse's nest**
> **someone's love letter**
> **was found**

> **just a little bite**
> **makes me dance—**
> **the red peppers**

Key 7: Compassion

Seeing and writing haiku is a way to practice care and compassion, and is a reminder to love nature as well as people. Haiku is a way to remember how everything is connected in our world, and if we feel connected, then we will not harm things, but rather care for them. The Dalai Lama said that a good way for kids to learn compassion is "to teach them to respect insects." If you can learn to care about something that is strange looking, tiny, and not easy to relate to, then you can realize that it shares the same "life" with human beings. The frog haiku shows the poet's attention to small creatures like a frog and the importance of it, even in the larger universe, the "ancient pond." The poet Basho made a haiku tradition in Japan that respected nature deeply, more than we do today. Haiku was often written about noticing and caring about tiny creatures. This was an idea taken from Buddhism in Japan, namely that we should not harm any creature, from humans down to insects. And that we should have compassion toward all creatures, because we are all a part of the same life force. In haiku, we can practice this compassion to connect to all living things. And we can take a step further to have compassion or a caring attitude toward even objects like our computer or toothbrush, treating everything in our environment with feeling and respect. Here are some examples of compassion in haiku:

after a hard rain
on a white orchid petal
a red ant in pain

—Nerissa B. Abrazaldo (age eleven, Philippines)

the grass awakens
convinced
night was weeping

—Serban-George Patriciu (age fourteen, Romania)

don't hit the fly—
he prays with his hands
and with his feet

—Kobayashi Issa (Japanese poet, 1763–1827)

■　　■　　■

If you can pay attention to these seven basic guidelines and practice them, you will be able to write good haiku. Maybe writing haiku cannot stop a war or a family fight, but being aware of these things and writing about them helps to keep a connection to nature and to other people. This can only help us, and our world, to be more relaxed and peaceful.

Arisa Jean San Nicolas (age twelve, Guam)

You have learned the importance of "seeing the world through haiku eyes" and connecting to nature and the world with an open heart. And now that you also know the Seven Keys to Writing Haiku, you are ready to start writing your first haiku. This chapter will get you started with some writing exercises. These nine easy activities will help you to write your first line, find good images, and understand the structure of haiku. But the very first step to writing haiku is reading a lot of good haiku.

project 1: writing your first haiku

First, Read Some Haiku

A haiku is not just a poem, but an experience. So in order to learn to write haiku, you must first *experience* haiku—that is, by reading other people's experiences that inspired them to write their haiku. You can then begin to write your own haiku experiences down on paper by following others' examples.

Since haiku are so short, they do not take long to read. You just need a few minutes. Sit down for a moment wherever you are, on a chair, on the grass, on a bus seat . . . just stop thinking about all the things you need to do, like homework, calling a friend, worrying about family, or what you want to eat or watch on television . . . just let all of that go and breathe deeply in and out for a moment . . . relax and breathe. Just focus on enjoying these haiku samples on the next few pages. Don't worry about their meanings or trying to figure them out. Remember to pause at least a few seconds between each haiku. Haiku are meant to help us relax and enjoy the ordinary moments around us. So sit back and enjoy these selections.

What You Need

Writing tools: pencil, pen, or calligraphy brush and ink; an eraser is handy

Paper: Your choice: It could be a little notebook (lined or unlined, as you like) to fit into your pocket, purse, or backpack. If you want to make a "small book" for your haiku, see page 57 for instructions.

in the rain
before the dawn: snails
migrating

—John Brandi (1943–)

sudden shower
in the empty park
swing still swinging

—Margaret Chula (1947–)

a dragonfly
peeks into
the empty torpedo

—Patricia Donegan (1945–)

all night
the sound of your breathing
the autumn wind

—Penny Harter (1940–)

Holding the water,
  held by it—
    the dark mud.

—William J. Higginson (1938–)

cinnamon wafts
of simmering apple-butter
attic hideaway

—Kris Kondo (1946–)

pausing
halfway up the stair —
white chrysanthemums

—Elizabeth Searle Lamb (1917–)

spring chill—
on short legs the sparrow
sips from Lake Ontario

—Bruce Ross (1945–)

sunlight is shining
warm on my back and I sit
heedless of all else

—Edith Shiffert (1916–)

summer storm
the spider's web
still there

—David Sutter (1943–)

Letting
    the cat in
    the fog in

—vincent tripi (1941–)

Lily
  out of the water . . .
    out of itself.

—Nicolas Virgilio (1928–1989)

a fallen blossom
flies back to the branch—
a butterfly

> —Arakida Moritake (1472–1549)

the stillness:
cicadas' voices
sink into stone

> —Matsuo Basho (1644–1694)

morning glory—
the well-bucket entangled
I ask for water

> —Chiyo-ni (Kaga No Chiyo, 1703–1775)

caught—
a firefly
in the mind's darkness

> —Yosa Buson (1716–1783)

the snail—
slowly, slowly
climbs Mt. Fuji

> —Kobayashi Issa (1763–1827)

a frog floating
in the water jar—
rain of summer

> —Masaoka Shiki (1867–1902)

after the riot
an amazingly beautiful
moonlit night

> —Kawahigashi Hekigodo (1873–1937)

round moon
round frozen lake
reflecting each other

> —Hashimoto Takako (1899–1963)

drawing light
from another world
the Milky Way

> —Ishihara Yatsuka (1919–1998)

summer grasses:
the wheels of a locomotive
come up to a stop

> —Yamaguchi Seishi (1901–1993)

above broken bricks
a butterfly
hangs out in the slums

> —Kaneko Tota (1919–)

one by one
he hands over the spring winds—
the balloon man

> —Sato Kazuo (1925–)

Spot Images

Good haiku have good images, which are things around us that make a picture. These images let us see and feel what the poet actually saw, so we can experience what the poet experienced as closely as possible. These images appeal to our senses. If we can learn to spot these images in haiku, we can get into the habit of seeing the images around us in our world, and then put more images in our own haiku. Look at the haiku you just read and find the images that relate to the senses. Add them to the list here:

seeing: a butterfly, _____, _____,

hearing: autumn wind, _____, _____

smelling: rain, _____, _____

tasting: apple-butter, _____, _____

touching: sunlight, _____, _____

Mostly we write about things that we can *see*, because they are the easiest to describe with words, so your seeing list will be longer than your other lists. Also, sometimes an image of something can appeal to many senses. For example, *rain* can appeal to almost all of our senses: seeing, hearing, smelling, touching, and sometimes even tasting.

Write Images

To write a good haiku you must have good images, so now we will practice writing images. Choose a word (such as *flower*, *car*, or *puppy*) and describe it in detail—to make the word something that you want the reader to see. I will start you off. For each word, try adding three images, each using more and more detail, as in these samples:

flower: a yellow daffodil, a yellow daffodil in the sun, a yellow daffodil in the sunny kitchen

your flower image: _____, _____,

_____

car: a red car, a red sports car, a waxed red Jaguar

your car image: _____, _____,

_____

puppy: a collie puppy, a collie puppy with white paws, a collie puppy with white paws running in the mud

your puppy image: _____, _____,

_____

Put Images Together

The next step is to put some of these images together. Haiku are usually about one main image, but they could have two, or even three at the most. Try putting your descriptive images together to form a haiku. This will be a practice haiku. You may find that you need to come up with a new image that connects with your first descriptive image. For example, we can take the daffodil flower

image and make it into the first two lines of a haiku. Then we could add another image for the last line, perhaps something strange or unusual. For example:

**yellow daffodil
in the sunny kitchen—
<u>a fly on a petal</u>**

Or the last line could be something else, like:

<u>no petals left by the cat</u>

or

<u>here come the ants</u>

Now, try creating your own haiku using your descriptive images.

Add to Others' Haiku

One way to learn to write good haiku is to use other people's haiku, even famous Japanese haiku. There are a few ways you can practice using others' haiku: You can simply use the first two lines of a haiku and write your own last line; you can substitute some words in a haiku with your own; you can use the last two lines of a haiku and write your own first line; or you can use just the first line of a haiku and write your own second and third lines. Here are some examples for practicing adding words to existing haiku:

Add the Last Line

**distant mountains
reflected in the eyes
<u>of a dragonfly</u>**

—Issa

**distant mountains
reflected in the eyes**

_____

**piano practice
through the open window
<u>the lilac</u>**

—Raymond Roseliep (American poet, 1917–1983)

**piano practice
through the open window**

_____

distant mountains
reflected in the <u>windshield</u>
<u>of father's car</u>

distant mountains
reflected in the _____
of _____

the <u>dragonfly</u>
peeks into
the <u>empty torpedo</u>

—Donegan

the <u>tiny spider</u>
peeks into
the <u>computer keys</u>

the _____
peeks into
the _____

<u>the butterfly</u>
is standing on tiptoes
at the ebbtide

—Chiyo-ni

_____
is standing on tiptoes
at the ebbtide

<u>After the rain</u>
a white butterfly
on the clothesline

—George Swede (American poet, 1941–)

_____
a white butterfly
on the clothesline

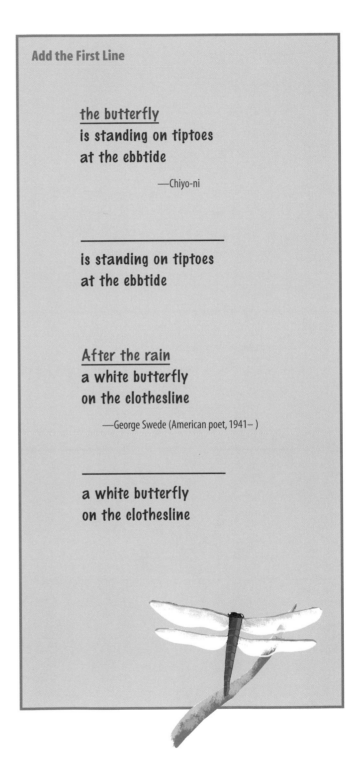

Add the Last Two Lines

summer grasses—
all that's left
of warriors' dreams

—Basho

summer grasses—
the wheels of a locomotive
come up to a stop

—Seishi

summer grasses—

_____

_____

Check Your Haiku

Now that you've written your first practice haiku, use the following checklist to make sure it has all of the elements it should have.

> 1. Is your haiku three lines, with or without a seventeen-syllable count, and one breath long?
>
> 2. Does your haiku have an image (a picture)?
>
> 3. Is there a kigo (season word) about nature?
>
> 4. Does it take place in the here and now (is it from a real experience)?
>
> 5. Does it express feeling (through the image)?
>
> 6. Is there a surprise ("ah!" moment)?
>
> 7. Does your haiku show compassion or connection to the world/nature?

When you write a haiku, use this checklist to see that you include *all* of the Seven Keys to Writing Haiku. Sometimes, even if you include some of these things (such as three lines and an image from nature), it still might not be a haiku. For example, you may be sad about seeing a dead bird or cat and write:

I am so sad
about seeing
the dead cat

This would *not* be a haiku. Why? Because it is explaining the feeling that you are sad. It doesn't use key #5: showing the feeling through an image.

24

Also, there is no strong image to make a picture of the meaning and feeling behind it. It would be better to use a strong image like this, which actually was from my real experience:

the dead cat's eyes
still shining
in the car's headlights

This would be a pretty good haiku, since it shows the sad feeling through the strong image of the "dead cat's eyes" "in the car's headlights." We feel the sadness, but still we need key #3: a kigo (word of nature), to make it a better haiku. We could add the season word *rainy* or *foggy*:

the dead cat's eyes
still shining
in the foggy headlights

Now this haiku has all seven of the keys needed to make a good haiku. Try going through the checklist after each haiku you write.

Write Your First Haiku from Your Experience

Now that you understand how to write with images, you know the Seven Keys to Writing Haiku, and you know how to make the haiku short (one breath in three lines), you are now ready to write your own haiku. But you must remember that it has to be from your real experience, or at least a memory of an experience you had.

First let me give an example of a recent experience I had and from which I wrote a few haiku. I was flying from Japan to America in January. I was sitting next to the window and I was taking a nap on the airplane for a few hours. When I woke up, I wanted to see if it was dark or light outside the window. So I lifted the shade and saw an amazing thing: There was a bright, full moon shining above the airplane. So I wrote a haiku sketch of the scene to show the feeling of beauty and surprise:

winter night—
on the wings of the plane
the moon's reflection

sitting on
the wings of the plane—
the icy Big Dipper

Be Open to the Haiku Moment

This reminds us that to write a haiku, the first thing is to have haiku eyes. Remember to include the moments of surprise in your haiku. These three steps may help guide you to a haiku:

Be open to the world around you;
See clearly what is there (the "ah!" moment);
Express the moment in a few words of a haiku (one breath long).

Hints for Writing the First Line

It is often a good idea to start with a nature image in the first line, perhaps something related to the season and weather of the day. In my haiku above, "winter night" is the first line. Or, in Basho's frog poem, the first line is "old pond—." Starting your haiku with a description of the season puts your mind into that mood and will help you to come up with images for that part of the year, so the rest of the haiku will easily follow. Starting the first line with nature will help you create an umbrella under which everything else will fall in place.

Hints for the Structure

One basic hint about the structure of a haiku is contrast. Sometimes a haiku is made by making a contrast, especially between the large and the small, or between big things in nature and the smaller world of humans and insects. This contrast makes a spark between the two images. Look at the two sample haiku below. Can you see the contrasting images of the bell and the butterfly? Now try to substitute these images with your own to create your own contrast of the great and the small.

> **on the temple bell**
> **sleeping peacefully,**
> **a butterfly**
>
> —Buson

> **on the Statue of Liberty**
> **sleeping peacefully**
> **a family of pigeons**

> **on the** _____
> **sleeping peacefully**
> **a** _____

Another haiku structure that is sometimes used is one of three lines that tells: "when," "where," and "what." This haiku by Basho shows this basic order:

> **autumn evening—** (when)
> **on a bare branch** (where)
> **a crow is sitting** (what)

Or, sometimes the line order is mixed:

> **on a bare branch** (where)
> **a crow is sitting—** (what)
> **autumn evening** (when)

Sometimes this form is not used at all, but it can be helpful to use this structure to get started. The main thing to remember is the "what," the main image of the haiku. For example, in Basho's haiku, the crow is the "what." Sometimes the "when" and the "where" are parts of the "what," like in the famous frog haiku: The "what" is the frog, and the "where" is the old pond, but the "when" is not told. However, we do know "when" it is happening because *frog* is a spring season word—so the "when" is in the springtime. As you practice more, you can try different ways of writing haiku. For your first few haiku, try using this basic order:

when *(give today's season/weather)* _____

where *(give the exact place)* _____

what *(give the main important thing)* _____

Another way to look at the structure of haiku is to see it as an upside-down triangle: the top is about nature in general or a certain space; the middle is about something happening in the space, in which you show a picture of the scene; and the bottom, at the point of the triangle, is the surprise element. This surprise in the last line brings the first and second lines together. In Basho's frog haiku, the *splash!* (the "sound of the water") brings it all together. Try writing your own haiku following this basic structure:

the space/nature _____
something within the space _____
surprise that brings it all together _____

Always remember Basho as an example:

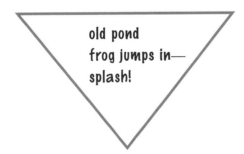

old pond
frog jumps in—
splash!

This is just one of many ways to write haiku—experiment and find your own ways.

Practice Creating Visual Forms of Haiku

You can have fun by trying different ways of writing haiku on the page, as in these examples:

Line Form and Spacing

Most poets line up the lines of their haiku on the left. Another popular way is the "step style" as in this example:

> quiet evening
>   the long sound
>   of the freight train fades

—Anita Virgil (American poet, 1931–)

Another style is the center the first and third lines to the middle line as in this haiku:

> bright sun
> the sheen of tall grasses
> when it bends

—Jim Kacian (American poet, 1953–)

Three Lines

> old pond—
> frog jumps in
> sound of the water

Some people have used two or four lines, but three seems best, to keep both the Japanese grouping of five, seven, and five syllables, and the kiriji (break in the haiku usually after the first or second line) here as the dash mark after "old pond," since this pause makes the feeling stronger.

One Line

old pond   frog jumps in   sound of the water

Here there are a few spaces between each group of words. Some feel that this is closer to the traditional Japanese way of writing a haiku in one line of calligraphy ink, though the Japanese would usually write in a vertical line down the page. Here are a few modern American examples of the one line haiku:

soaking up   the moon   the snail

—Alexis Rotella (American poet, 1947–)

beyond the sink   of undone dishes   bird feeder

—Marlene Mountain (American poet, 1939–)

Eye-ku or Visual Haiku

frog

j
u
m
p
s

old   P   in   D

O

N

. . . sound of the water

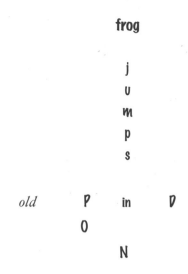

This haiku connects to our eye: It makes a picture or image of what the haiku is about. It is often made in the shape of what the poem is about, like the letters made in a circle for the word, "pond" and the words "frog jumping in" dropping into it on the page. And like modern abstract art, some people have even tried writing a visual haiku by using only *one* word as in this "haiku":

tundra

—Cor van den Heuvel (American poet, 1931–)

It is certainly not a traditional haiku, but it is an interesting and playful "one-word haiku": here the "tundra" is the very top of a high rocky mountain where there is nothing growing like trees, and there is only empty sky—which is seen in the white space around the word on the page. You can also enjoy experimenting with visual haiku. This might be done more easily and freely with a pencil or paints, unless you can do computer graphics. Try your hand at it—it's fun!

Loon

the old pond (3 words)
the frog jumps into it (5 words)
sound of water (3 words)

This modern American form always uses three words, five words, and then three words, which tries to keep the rhythm of the Japanese haiku of the five-seven-five-syllable count, and so the middle line is longer. This makes a nice balance when you look at it, but sometimes it can sound a little awkward.

Last, Just Practice

By now you have written some haiku exercises as well as your very own haiku. This is a good beginning. It can be fun and rewarding, but it takes practice, like learning anything else, from playing baseball to using a computer. So practice every day or as often as you can. The more you practice haiku seeing and writing, the easier it will get. Keep your pencil or pen and little notebook with you at all times, so you can immediately record the little haiku moments you see around you. As a writer of haiku, you are like a reporter: You are reporting important news to the world about little things that most people might not stop and see. You just have to look and write it down as soon as you see and feel it. Basho said there should be no gap between experiencing the haiku moment and the writing of it—like "the striking of lightning." It is not something you have to think too much about if you are awake to your world. The haiku will just be there if you are there.

squatting
the frog observes
the clouds

—Chiyo-ni

Haiku are about nature, so when you write haiku you are also developing your own relationship with nature. This chapter focuses on nature in haiku. Through the next four activities you'll find tips on adding images of nature to your haiku. You'll also create your own season word dictionary and discover nature walks as inspiration for your haiku writing.

We say that haiku are about nature, but we often see that haiku are about people, love, war, and other subjects—all of these things are always a part of nature. In Japan, nature includes all things, because the Japanese see everything, even our human life, as a part of nature. It is like nature is the umbrella and everything in our world is under it. This idea first came out of Japan's Shinto religion, which believes that everything in nature is alive and has a *kami*, or spirit: Every single person, frog, and bird, and every rock and tree, is alive and has a spirit. Later this idea was made stronger by the Japanese Buddhist religion, which believes that everything in this world is sacred: The sky, the sparrow, the grass, the snake, and the ant are just as important as a human. This belief that all creatures—from humans to insects—are connected is the true spirit of haiku.

tired
by the crowd of children—
a sparrow

—Issa

project 2: your favorite season haiku

What You Need

Writing tools: pencil, pen, or calligraphy brush and ink; an eraser is handy

Paper: Any paper you find will be fine, such as a paper napkin, envelope, or scrap paper, or a nice little notebook for your nature walks. If you want to make a small book for your season haiku, see page 57 for instructions.

This is why so many haiku are about nature, and our relationship to nature. That is also why there are so many haiku about little creatures, such as fireflies and frogs. And remember what the haiku poet Basho said about haiku about nature: "If you want to write about the pine, you must become one with the pine"—that is, you have to feel that close to nature in order to write about it. If we can do that, we would not harm our environment or creatures in it, for it is a part of us. Haiku is a small way to stop this destruction—by connecting more to nature.

In old times, the Japanese thought so much about the importance of nature and the seasons that when they made a poetry book, they grouped the poems by the season. This became an important custom that is still used today, especially in haiku books.

Cyril Dautigny (age twelve, France)

Basho's Teaching on Nature

> above the stream
> chasing her reflection
> the dragonfly

—Cyril Dautigny (age twelve, France)

Basho, the great haiku master, always gave his haiku students this advice to follow nature. He often instructed students to write or sketch from nature in their haiku. A few hundred years later, Shiki, a haiku poet, named this on-the-spot sketch

a *shasei*. Here is a famous story about Basho and one of his students that shows how to make a true sketch of nature. One sunny autumn day, Basho and some of his students were walking through the rice fields together. Now and then they would stop and write some haiku about what they saw. Basho's best student, Kikaku, rushed over to Basho. He showed Basho a haiku that he had just written and was proud of:

> take wings off
> a dragonfly—
> a red pepper

When Basho saw Kikaku's haiku he said, "No, this is not a good haiku—because you kill the dragonfly. If you want to make a good haiku, you must give it life and say instead:

31

```
add wings
to a red pepper—
a dragonfly
```

Of course, Kikaku was being clever, because there are red dragonflies in Japan in autumn. And if they had no wings they could look like red peppers. But to write a good haiku, you need more than cleverness: You need compassion toward nature. So this was a great message to Basho's students about the importance of nature and the importance of our attitude toward nature.

Write an "I Remember Nature" Haiku

Now that you are familiar with the importance of nature in haiku, try to write your own haiku about an experience you had with nature. Think of a time when you felt close to nature or close to a small creature in nature. Say to yourself, "I remember . . ." and some memory or image will come to your mind. "I remember . . . walking in the springtime." Maybe you were outside taking a walk in early spring. There was a pale blue sky and bright sun, and you could smell the soil under your feet, and see some green buds coming out on the winter trees. Maybe you can remember seeing something in nature, like the clouds or a bird. Perhaps you remember suddenly hearing the honking of geese overhead and looking up to see a V shape flying back for the warm spring. These could all be haiku moments. Try to remember an

experience in nature when you noticed something that captured your whole attention. What was the season, and what was the main subject in nature that you are writing about? Write a haiku about this moment:

_____

_____

_____

Take a Ginko Walk

Another way to find a haiku moment is to take a walk outside. This is called a *ginko* in Japanese. A ginko is a special walk in nature when you write haiku about what you see. So put your pen and little notebook in your pocket, backpack, or purse, and open your eyes, relax, and start walking. You can take a short walk for only fifteen minutes or a long walk of an hour or two. Every now and then, stop and sit down to observe things more closely. Just relax, look, and feel what you see. Perhaps it is summer. Look down and see the ladybug crawling on a grass blade. Look up and see the clouds passing the skyscrapers. Describe these nature images. For example, these images could make a haiku moment of noticing big nature and small creatures. It shows the mixing of nature's world and our human world. The word telling the season is the season word. Here it would be *ladybug* for the summer season:

```
clouds pass
by skyscrapers—
a ladybug asleep
```

Describe whatever hits you deeply. Don't forget to use a season word. Write these haiku moments down on the paper quickly as you see and feel them.

_____

_____

_____

Writing five to ten haiku about the same thing is a great practice. Try using different words to describe the same experience. For example, make other haiku using the same images:

```
clouds crash
into skyscrapers—
ladybug asleep on a grass blade
```

season words: ladybug, grass blade (for summer)

```
summer breeze—
clouds crash
into skyscrapers
```

season word: summer breeze (for summer)

Now try several more of your own:

_____

_____

_____

season word: _____

_____

_____

_____

season word: _____

The Japanese Saijiki (Season Word Dictionary)

We know that when people write haiku, they often write about the season, but did you know that they don't usually say the season directly? For example, instead of writing "the autumn season," they would use a season word, or kigo, that would hint at the season. For example, the words *geese, chrysanthemum, fog,* and *dragonfly* are part of the autumn season. So when these words appear in a haiku, we know it takes place in autumn. More than three hundred years ago, the Japanese collected these season words into a book, a "season word dictionary," or *saijiki*. Most haiku poets even today have a saijiki to help them write haiku.

```
```

Every country and every region has its own kind of weather and seasons. So each country in the world would have to create its own saijiki. You don't have to have a saijiki, but it might be fun and useful. Perhaps you could even make your own mini-saijiki, or list of words. In the saijiki, each season has seven different grouping of things: the season's weather, the heavens, the earth, humanity, observances, animals, and plants. Here is an example from each group for *autumn*. Practice by adding your own season words to this list:

1. the season's weather (climate): chilly, _____, _____

2. the heavens (in sky, space): harvest moon, _____, _____

3. the earth (geography): flower field, _____, _____

4. humanity (human life, activities): scarecrow, _____, _____

5. observances (holidays): Halloween, _____, _____

6. animals (also birds, insects): cricket, _____, _____

7. plants (also flowers, trees): maple leaves, _____, _____

Now that you've had some practice with the saijiki, in your notebook you can make a new list of the seven groups for your own favorite season.

Choose one season: spring, summer, autumn, or winter:

Your Favorite Season: Mini-Saijiki for the Season of

_____

the season's weather: _____, _____, _____

the heavens: _____, _____, _____

the earth: _____, _____, _____

humanity: _____, _____, _____, _____

observances: _____, _____, _____

animals: _____, _____, _____, _____

plants: _____, _____, _____

To study further about the traditional Japanese mini-saijiki for the four seasons, see the renga project chapter, especially page 51.

Write a Haiku about Your Favorite Season

Spring and autumn are probably the two most popular seasons in Japan, and so most haiku are written about these seasons, especially about cherry blossoms for spring and maple leaves for autumn. Here is a famous haiku about the *autumn* season. I will explain the season words and their meaning.

> beautiful—
> after the typhoon
> the red peppers
>
> —Buson

season word: typhoon (for autumn)

This haiku was written by Yosa Buson, who lived three hundred years ago. He was also a painter, so his haiku have good images, like in a painting. Usually only one season word is used, but in this haiku there are actually two kigo: the main kigo is *typhoon* (autumn storm) and the other one is *red peppers*. Here is a beautiful image of the red peppers in the quiet morning sunlight. The quiet is felt more strongly after the windy storm, or typhoon, is over, and the haiku makes a good contrast between the greatness of nature in the big storm and the small bright red peppers. After the storm, the peppers look brighter, for then everything is clearer against the blue sky. The haiku is good because it makes us feel the power of nature and notice the small beauty that we often miss. Also, it shows the poet's sense of "ah!" when he suddenly found the beautiful red peppers in the bare autumn field after the storm.

Now take a look at your saijiki. What are some words that describe your favorite season? Try to write a haiku that shows why you like this season. Think of a memory of that season and write about something that happened in that season that you cannot forget. And if your favorite season happens to be the season you are in now, you can take a ginko walk, or you can write about something you see outside your window. Remember, it is best if you can write from memory or real experience.

_____

_____

_____

season word: _____

Now write a haiku about something special about your favorite season, perhaps a beautiful surprise you saw in nature, like in the red pepper haiku:

_____

_____

_____

season word: _____

And now write a haiku about some sad surprise you saw in nature, like in these haiku:

violets have grown
among the ruins
of my burned house

—Yagi Shokyu-ni (Japanese poet, 1713–1781)

season word: violets (for spring)

dying cicada—
not showing it
in its song

—Basho

season word: cicada (for summer)

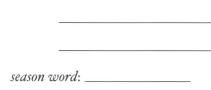

season word: _____

So when writing haiku about nature, there is always something to give you inspiration to write. And at the same time it gives you a feeling of connection to the world around you, for we are all a part of nature—haiku gives us a way to write about that experience.

So far we know that haiku are poems of three lines, with or without a seventeen-syllable count, and usually about nature. But there are also other writing forms related to haiku. Here we'll explore a haiku-related form called *haibun*. This form lets us add a story to enhance our poem or it lets us add a poem to enhance a story. Here are some examples of haibun:

All creatures, even fleas and lice, have life force. And they are dear to one another like people are. And it is bad to kill any living thing, especially when they make a family.

> swimming
> captured in a tub
> the fish enjoy the cool water

—Issa (from *The Year of My Life*, 1819)

When I was little I often played by myself. I didn't play with the other children much because they sometimes made fun of me after my mother died. So I used to go into the backyard and sit by the woodpile and cry. And I wrote this haiku:

> come here
> sparrows without mothers
> and play with me

—Issa (when eight years old)

Every haiku is a piece of a story. It is not a whole story, but a hint of a story that the reader completes in his or her own mind. The haiku just tells one little moment, one little happening that only lasts a few seconds—as long as one breath. The splash of a frog in a pond, the siren of a police car in the quiet

project 3: your haibun (story with haiku)

What You Need

Writing tools: pencil, pen, or calligraphy brush and ink; an eraser is handy

Paper: Choose a special large-sized notebook with lined or unlined paper. A small notebook would be fine, but for stories and haiku you may wish to have a bigger notebook, diary, or journal. You can also make a "small book" (see page 57 for instructions) for your haibun.

night, hail hitting on top of your head, a cricket crying under a soldier's helmet, a swallow coming out of the nose of a big Buddha statue, violet flowers in the ashes of a burned house. When we see something surprising, we usually say, "oh!" or "ah!" and that is the haiku moment—something that is happening around us right now. You just have to be still and wait, to catch the mini haiku story.

If this story behind the haiku is told, it becomes something else. This mixing of a story and a haiku is called a *haibun*. In Japanese, *hai* means "haiku" and *bun* means "prose" (story or sentences). Long before Basho lived, it was a Japanese custom to mix poetry and story, but it was Basho who made the haibun form famous.

Yet haibun are not whole stories; haibun are just pieces of stories. A haibun can be just a few sentences, or it can be a few paragraphs. It can be a sketch of a scene, an impression, a diary entry, or a longer series of travel journals. Usually the story part is given first, and then the haiku comes at the end; or sometimes the story and the haiku are mixed. The haiku does not repeat what is in the story, but instead the haiku completes the story or makes it deeper. The haiku still needs to be strong and something that could stand by itself. When the story and haiku are put together well they make a haibun.

Your Own Haibun Diary

Something fun and special to do is to keep a "haibun diary": a record of the important things that you experience with your impressions. Every day, or at least once a week, try to write a haibun describing a moment you experienced, ending it with a haiku. Try this for a month, a season, or even a year. You can start with any subject—perhaps start describing your day. But first think of something that moved your heart, something that you saw and felt during the day . . . some image, some sound, something. . . . This is a chance to practice seeing with haiku eyes, so keep your eyes and heart open to the world around you. Then recording what you see will be simple. Your haibun doesn't have to be perfect. It is just for you, so that you can write honestly about what you really think and feel. You do not have to pretend—you can write whatever you want. Writing in a real way will make good haibun and will be a very special diary. You will find that you will learn many things about yourself and the world. Remember, nothing is too big or small, too good or bad, or too happy or sad for haiku or haibun. It can include all of life. Haibun is a chance for you to tell more of your own story behind the haiku moments you experience in your life every day.

A Short Diary Entry

This is a short diary entry by Basho about his poor living situation. Sometimes he did not have much food to eat. He wrote this haibun about his situation.

The rich eat plenty of meat. And even the strong farmers have vegetables. But I am so poor:

> snowy morning—
> alone, chewing
> dried salmon

You can write your own short haibun about something that is upsetting you. It is like a secret diary entry. Write it in your notebook or special diary.

A Short Impression

This is also a short diary impression by Basho:

Sora [my close friend] is living next to my hut. So in the morning and night we visit each other. When I fix food he helps me with the wood for the fire. On nights when I make tea he sometimes knocks on my door. He usually likes to be alone and quiet. But one night he visited me in the snow:

> you, make a fire
> I'll show you something nice—
> a snowball

Think of something nice that happened with a friend. Write a short sketch about it in your notebook or diary.

Your Travel Journal

The longer haibun are often diaries of a journey, written while traveling, such as Basho's famous *Oku no Hosomichi (Narrow Road to the Deep North)*. This is a record of Basho's travels on foot and horseback through the villages and mountains of northern Japan. He traveled almost the entire year of 1689. Many of Basho's famous haiku were actually taken from his travel diaries, or his haibun. For example, the famous haiku about the sadness of war was taken from this haibun:

In the village Komatsu we visited Tada Shrine. There we saw the helmet of a great samurai named Sanemori (1111–1183). And we saw a piece from his armor clothes. They were given to him by the feudal lord, Yoshitomo of the Genji clan. It was a special helmet. It was decorated all over with gold flowers. And at the top was a dragon's head between two horns. After the samurai was killed in battle, a friend Yoshinaka wrote a prayer. And another friend Jiro carried the prayer with the samurai's helmet and things to the shrine. This story was written on the shrine wall.

> sad, underneath
> a samurai's helmet
> a cricket crying

Basho ended this haibun story with the haiku about the cricket under the helmet. It makes us feel the sadness of the soldier's death and the sadness of war.

Basho's haiku is not a summary of the story's background. He takes one or two strong images from the story and then adds a little something to the story, making a nice balance between the story and the haiku poem. The haiku ending is just the catching of that one little sound of the cricket crying under the helmet, but it creates a big, deep feeling.

A Long Travel Sketch

You can now write a one-paragraph diary entry about something that you saw when you were traveling on a trip or even within your own hometown. It could be about a special family vacation or a school field trip. Your haibun could also be about something sad you saw, like in Basho's story that you just read. Write it in your special notebook.

A Short Travel Sketch of a Scene

Here is a short sketch of scenery by Basho:

One day I spent a whole day by the seaside and enjoyed it so much. Suddenly I realized it was getting dark:

> **the sea darkens:**
> **the voices of the ducks**
> **faintly white**

You can now make your own short sketch of a scene about something you enjoyed seeing. Record it in your notebook.

Here is another short travel sketch also by Basho:

I wrote this while I was riding on horseback on my trip:

> **by the roadside**
> **the white mallow flower**
> **was eaten by my horse**

You can see that even in the haibun, the haiku still contain season words: *cool water, sparrows, snowy morning, snowball, cricket, ducks, white mallow flower.*

Now make your own short sketch about an unusual or funny thing that happened to you while traveling.

Overall, writing haibun gives you a chance to tell the story behind your haiku experiences—for some people haiku are too short to describe a haiku moment. For this reason, haibun may also make the writing of haiku a lot easier. Haibun is also a wonderful practice for writing haiku.

Since haiku are like brush paintings with words, it became a custom in Japan to add real paintings to haiku. These became known as *haiga*. Haiga art combines haiku and painting on the same paper. You have already discovered how to add strong images to your haiku with words. In this chapter you can add new life to your haiku by creating pictures and paintings to illustrate those same images.

A haiku is said to be a tiny sketch in words—the capture of a tiny moment with a tiny image, such as the frog in Basho's famous poem, or like in another of his haiku:

> sticking to a mushroom
> the leaf
> from an unknown tree

We can see the image clearly: a mushroom with a leaf on it. It is a simple image. If we sketched it, it would take only a few brush strokes. Haiku are really tiny "word paintings" of things that simply happen, like the leaf on the mushroom. As in life, things happen and surprise us—suddenly a leaf blown from somewhere sticks to a mushroom, or a caterpillar crawls on the mushroom, or a deer munches the mushroom, or a bird poops on the mushroom. All of these tiny moments are pictures that can be a haiku. Readers imagine and complete the pictures in their minds.

It has long been a tradition in Japan, China, and Korea to put all kinds of poetry and paintings on the same page. From these long-ago times, haiku was painted in one line or three parts down the page, using a calligraphy brush and black ink on the white paper. Sometimes the poet would do both the painting and the haiku. Sometimes the poet would write the poem on an artist friend's painting. Or sometimes the artist would

project 4:
your haiga (drawing and haiku)

What You Need

Writing tools: pencil, pen, paintbrush, calligraphy brush and ink; an eraser is handy; watercolors, crayons, or colored pencils.

Paper: Any white, unlined paper, or any sized blank notebook, would be fine for haiga, but you may wish to have a bigger notepad, sheets of art paper, or a blank diary or journal for your artwork. You can also make a "small book" (see page 57 for instructions) for your haiga.

artist

Basho. *There, in the Old Pond.* Hanging
scroll, 22.8 by 52.5 cm. Ink
monochrome on paper.

make a painting to go with the poet's poem. From
the seventeenth century, when haiku became popular, people started doing haiga. People began putting haiku and pictures together. These sketches or
paintings were sometimes done with black ink (as
calligraphy). These black ink paintings were called
sumie paintings, and sometimes the paintings were
done with watercolors. Yet the sketch was usually
simple. Of course, the color paintings filled in the
paper more. The black ink paintings used only a
few brush strokes, as the haiku itself is like a few
brush strokes creating one main image of a flower,
frog, or bird. With a few brush strokes and a haiku
of a few words, a mini-world unfolds.

First, Look at Some Haiga

Look at the Japanese haiga paintings on this page.
You can see the image of the frog by the pond in

Basho's famous haiku and the image of the flying
swallow in Issa's haiku. This kind of haiga, with
only simple brush strokes, became most popular in
the seventeenth century, and is still popular today.
Sometimes haiga is called Zen art, as it is one of
the art practices to keep us in the present moment.
Haiga use two ways—through haiku words and
brush strokes—to help bring our minds back to the
now: the *splash!* of water, the little bird flying alone.
These painted images make the haiku stronger, and
the haiku words make the painting stronger. The
painting and the words work together. Haiga help
us to see the haiku more deeply.

Now look at the haiga on pages 43–45. These
are haiga done by children from all over the world.
These are in color, but some were also in black ink.
From these samples you can get a good idea of how

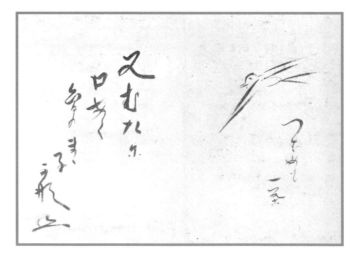

Issa. *Swallow.* Hanging scroll, 29.9 cm by 44.8 cm.
Ink monochrome on paper.

The waves lick my feet
As I sit on the cool beach
And watch the sunset

Rebecca Radford (New Zealand)

images of an arrow or cat, or abstract lines. Ever since ancient times, even before language and paper were invented, people created art. Humans made marks on stones, cave walls, wood, bones, and palm leaves. They made images of animals, insects, birds, and people: everything in nature.

Now you can enjoy making a tiny sketch to go with your own haiku, or you can do a sketch or painting to go with a well-known haiku, or a friend's haiku. You can use a pencil, pen, paintbrush, permanent marker, crayon, or chalk—any writing tool you like. You can use any kind of paper (unlined is best) that you like—computer paper, art paper, cardboard, or a notebook to sketch in. You can use any size paper: big or small, square or

to do your own haiga. The children's haiga make their haiku more alive and interesting, don't you think?

Your Own Haiga

How many times do we doodle on paper, almost without knowing it? We sketch circles, boxes,

Yui Itakaru (Japan)

さんまさん
ピカピカ光って
切れそうだ

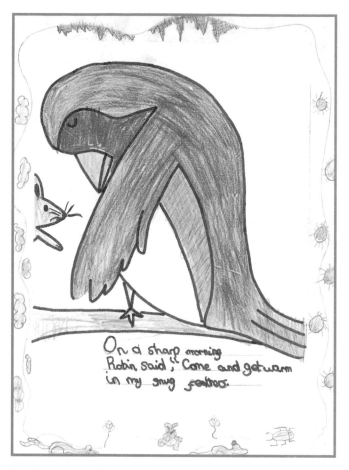

On a sharp morning
Robin said," Come and get warm
in my snug feathers.

Stacy Brown (age nine, United Kingdom)

on the spot about something you noticed today, making sure to include the season. Notice the most important image or images in the haiku. Notice the feeling or mood of the haiku, since you put not only the image, but also the mood of the image (happy or sad, for example) into the haiga. Pause to feel the image and the mood of the haiku together, as a guide to start drawing.

Take the paper and writing tool and start drawing on the paper. Follow your heart, and remember that there is no right or wrong when drawing a picture—it is just expression, marks on paper. First let it be a simple sketch—only a few brush strokes will be fine. As you practice, some time you may want to try something more filled in, using colored paints. Now add your haiku to the sketch or painting. Put it where it can be seen (letters not too big or small), and let it make a good balance on the paper with the sketch or painting

As practice, try several different haiga with the same haiku. Keep these haiga in a special note-book, hang them on the wall, or throw them away if you like. For example, put the haiga on a long strip of paper and hang it from a string tied to a tree or bell outside. Or share these haiga with friends and family, write and draw them with others, or give them away to others. Enjoy these haiku moments—and your own creativity!

square or round, or long strips. You may want to sketch the image first and then add the haiku, or do the reverse.

Here are some guidelines to get you started: Sit down and relax, take a few deep breaths . . . feel the chair, the room, the space. Take a haiku (yours or another's) and read it carefully, or write a haiku

Haiga for a Haiku Series
or Haibun Series

You could also do a haiku series, called a *gunsaku* (of six to twelve haiku), about one theme—for example "Nature Images of Peace"—and you could make haiga drawings to go with it. You could also do a haiku sequence, called a *rensaku* (of six to twelve haiku), consisting of a story with a beginning, middle, and end, on a particular subject such as "The Whale's Journey," and then you could illustrate it with haiga.

Lidia de Jesus Morales Sanchez (age eleven, Mexico)

Imee Marie C. Nazari (age ten, Guam)

You could also take one of your haibun (story and haiku) and add a haiga illustration to make it more interesting. Or you could make a collection of six to twelve haibun about different things you experienced or of a series of haibun from a trip you took.

Use your experience and imagination to express your world through haiga. Haiga is not only fun to do, but it is powerful, because you use both the power of words and the power of the drawing to communicate to others. The word and the picture together make a very strong impression.

first winter shower—
the kite bird
fixes its feathers

—Kyorai

the strong wind
whirls the leaves down

—Basho

slacks are wet
from stream wading
this morning

—Boncho

this frightens the badgers
in the thin bamboo forest...

—Fumikuni

project 5: your renga (linked poetry)

— *Patricia Donegan with Kris Kondo*

Τhis is the beginning of a Japanese *renga*, or linked poem. This one is from the renga "Winter's First Shower" from *Monkey's Raincoat*, written in 1691. Renga is written by a group of people. As you can see in the above renga, people take turns to write their own part of two or three lines and then link all of the lines together to create one long linked poem. This is a great way to create a group poem with friends.

Renga was a very popular form of poetry in the fourteenth century, and it is becoming popular again today. Basho's friends would get together to have a renga party. It would be a relaxing time when they could share moments together. At these parties, two or more people would write a long, chain-linked poem. Each person took a turn adding two or three lines, like in the above renga. At that time, this practice was called *haikai no renga*, which was Basho's unique style of renga. Renga is also the

What You Need

Writing tools: pencil, pen, or calligraphy brush and ink; an eraser is handy

Paper: Any white lined or unlined paper, or any size notebook, would be fine, but for renga you may wish to have a bigger notepad or sheets of paper, or even a renga diary or journal for group poetry. You can also make a "small book" (see page 57 for instructions) for your group renga.

Americn word for any linked verse. But if we write in Basho's linked style today, we call it *renku*.

Actually, you may be surprised to learn that Basho was not really a haiku poet, but in fact a renku poet! When he was alive, people did not write individual haiku; they wrote renku together in a group. But sometimes they would practice by themselves making some *hokku*, the opening three lines of the renku. They did this to prepare for the parties, to make a good beginning for the poem. The hokku had to be a greeting to the party's host and to the place. It also had to have a season feeling—something about nature. This set the mood for the entire group poem. So what we think are Basho's haiku are really hokku from his group poems, or his haibun (stories with haiku), or haiga paintings. You see, the word *haiku* was not even a word in Japanese until the late nineteenth century, about two hundred years after Basho died. Later, a poet named Shiki (1867–1902) took the first three lines—the hokku—and started writing them alone. He made haiku a poem completely separate from haikai no renga. He called these three lines *haiku*. That's the story of how haiku was born from linked poetry, which has been known as renku since that time.

But there is a little more to the story. The renga group poetry came out of an even older form of poetry called *tan-renga*, which was a linked poem done by only two people, usually friends or a couple. One person wrote the first three lines and the other person answered with the last two lines, making a nice exchange. The two parts made five lines (of five-seven-five-seven-seven syllable groupings, or thirty-one-syllables) altogether. This five-line poem was called *waka* (later, *tanka*) poetry. It is the oldest form of poetry in Japan and was written from the eighth century on. The upper-class people of the court wrote this kind of poetry, mostly about nature and love. Later, this social group poetry became popular among common people. The renga was really the act of linking waka together.

Look again at the sample by Basho's group. The first person, Kyorai, wrote three lines of five-seven-five Japanese syllables about the kite bird, and then the next person, Basho, wrote two lines of seven seven Japanese syllables about the strong wind. This made one complete waka poem. The parts are linked and describe the same windy winter rain. These two friends, Basho and Kyorai, made two links, and then their other friends added more parts of waka until there was a long chain poem of thirty-six links, called a *kasen*. Some groups even made one hundred, one thousand, or even ten thousand links! Today people usually don't have time to write so much, so most renku groups make poems with twenty, eighteen (half of a kasen), or only twelve links, called a *shisan*. To start, try to write a group poem of twelve links with friends. Today most people outside of Japan know about haiku, but fewer know about renku. But when they find out about it and try it, they like it so much. Why? Well, renku is a fun social art and that creates harmony and good feeling among people—and this is something we need more of in this world.

The Importance and Way of Za

First of all, you need to make a *za*, a group or circle of friends for writing renku. This is the group spirit of renku. Choose a relaxing place indoors, or outdoors in nature. The za, or group of at least two or more people, sits in a circle around a table with pencils or pens and a pile of paper to write with. You can enjoy sharing the room, snacks, and drinks together. Remember to respect each other's creativity—this is a shared poem, not a contest.

Take turns and write a long group poem together. Each person writes a link of two or three lines, as many times as you can go around the circle. Use the chart for the *shisan* (twelve-link renku) as a guide (see pages 52–53). There are many ways to do shisan, but this chart will guide you on how to write each link: what season to write about (spring, summer, autumn, or winter), writing with no season at all, or something special to include in the link, like the moon, a flower, or love.

This group renku will probably take about two hours, but you can be as slow or as fast as you like. One person in the group could write or type up the whole renku to give, mail, or e-mail later to the others in the group.

In Japan, the group always has a leader called a *sabaki* to keep track of what goes on in the renku. The leader helps the group with the three tools to help everyone write: the renku topic checklist, the saijiki (season word dictionary), and the form charts, such as for the shisan. If there is no leader, you can still use these tools to help you. These tools are covered later in this chapter.

The Three Pointers to Writing Renku

Pointer One: Form

Renku is a chain-linked poem. But it is *not* a story, since it has no beginning, middle, and end. Instead, it is like pieces of a jigsaw puzzle. Actually, one Japanese renku poet and scholar, Tadashi Kondo, calls it "a jigsaw puzzle of the universe." Why? Well, renku can include anything and everything, from small daily things like grandmother's chair, a favorite T-shirt, a pet cat, a scary dream, a cell phone, or a friend's secret; to big world things like a peace treaty, the cut rainforests, homeless people in cities, or solar-powered cars; to natural and cosmic things like a bee on a shoe, a beached whale, stars on a summer night, a space shuttle, or the Milky Way. You can write about anything in renku. Both human things and things of nature are in the universe's jigsaw puzzle.

And of course you do not know which piece of

the puzzle you will pick next. There is no special order in renku, like there is in a story. In renku, anything can pop up at any time. It is like you are in an airplane or are a bird flying: You see many surprising things as you pass by, like misty clouds, the half moon, snowy mountains, green forests, a herd of antelope running over a field, the blue lights of a city, or tiny houses in circles. There is no order, just the flow of sights as you pass. So, as you write renku, you follow the landscape of your mind or imagination, and the group's imagination. All you have to do is to link your popped-up words with the others' in the group.

Renku poetry has a good mix of images from nature's world and our human world. You have to use season words and nature images, but you also have to use subjects from our everyday human world. This makes the "jigsaw puzzle of the universe."

Pointer Two: Link

To make a chain, we need links, as one link has to connect to another. In order to link your poem lines, you'll have to listen to what the other person wrote before you. You do not know what the person will say, so it is a surprise. And what you write will be a surprise for the person after you. Try to connect what you write to what the person before you wrote. For example, in Basho's poem, the first link introduced the "winter shower," so the next person made a link by saying the "strong wind," since cold rain usually has a strong wind. This is a link. One way to

make a connection is through a season word or nature image. But about half of the links are "no season" links—so then you link with a topic, as in the shisan example on page 53: #9 link having the autumn "season word" "scarecrow" is linked by #10's "no season" word the "barn door." Also, in traditional Japanese renga, even the season order was not followed. But in the twelve-link renku—shisan—that you will try, there is a basic season order to follow, and this way of linking is easiest.

Pointer Three: Shift

To make a poem interesting, it needs variety. The poem needs to change sometimes—that is, change the topic or direction so that it is not always about the same thing. Sometimes we do not just link and connect, but instead take a leap. This is where we can introduce any topic we want. For example, in Basho's renga, the third link makes a shift from the winter rain and wind to the "slacks" "wet from stream wading." Perhaps after the rainstorm it was a clear day and good for wading in the water. A checklist of topics is often used so that a variety of topics can be covered.

Three Tools for Writing Renku

Tool One: A Checklist of Topics

Use a checklist to make the renku more interesting and to help you think of things to write about. These are not a set of "rules," but rather a guide.

A checklist of about fifty words like *wind, sports, religion, calamity, travel, birds,* and *drinks* will help you to include a variety of topics in your renku. Try not to use the actual topic words, but instead use your own "jigsaw puzzle pieces." For example, for the topic word *wind* use a more exact word, like *hurricane* or *gentle breeze*; for the topic word *calamity* use a phrase like *bombs dropping* or *flash floods*; and for the topic word *drink* use *hot chocolate* or *icy cola*. If you use only the topic words themselves, your renku will be boring, so try to cover as many of the topics—using your own made-up words—as much as you can. For one renku, try to use at least one topic from each of the ten boxes and use as many topics as you can for one renku. It is fun to mix topics, as in the made-up words "student-protests"—which covers two topics, *study* and *current events*. See the checklist of ten topics below:

A RENKU TOPIC CHECKLIST

[1]	[2]	[3]	[4]	[5]
heavenly body _____	mountain/hill _____	beast _____	tree _____	god _____
falling weather _____	field _____	bird _____	grass/wildflower _____	God/Buddha/Allah _____
rising weather _____	waterfront _____	insect _____	crops _____	religion _____
wind _____		fish _____	plants _____	
sun/moon _____			blossom /flower _____	

[6]	[7]	[8]	[9]	[10]
hard life _____	dream _____	people _____	building _____	current event _____
sickness _____	nostalgia _____	body part _____	study/learning _____	historical event _____
calamity _____	mood _____	occupation _____	game _____	scheduled event _____
accident _____	apparition _____	clothing _____	music _____	
(transience) change _____	color _____	food _____	art _____	
	number _____	drink _____	drama _____	
	fragrance _____	instrument/equipment _____	sports _____	
			travel vehicle _____	
			place name _____	
			person's name _____	
			foreign country _____	

Tool Two: A Mini-Saijiki
(Season Word Dictionary)

The saijiki was first discussed in the Your Favorite Season Haiku chapter. The saijiki is even more useful when writing renku. Since you use a saijiki to include good nature images, the saijiki is really the most important tool. Usually the leader helps keep track of the topics from the checklist, but everyone can use their own saijiki themselves. Using the saijiki is not a rule for renku, but it may help you think of nature words to use for a certain season, like the season words *snow sledding* or *icicle* for the winter season. Sometimes a season word overlaps a topic checklist word you might come up with. For example, for the topic "bird" you might use *robin,* which is also a season word for spring—at once you can cover the topic checklist word and the season word. And of course for the season word you can also use any nature words you want to—you can make them up. But if you want some help to start, see this mini-saijiki listing.

MINI-SAIJIKI FOR THE FOUR SEASONS

THE SEASON	spring	summer	autumn	winter
THE WEATHER	warm long day	hot muggy	chilly long night	freezing short day
THE HEAVENS	misty moon late frost mist	cool moon billowing clouds thunder	harvest moon fall colors Milky Way	frozen moon snow north wind
THE EARTH	spring sea spring mud melting snow	waterfall summer meadow green fields	autumn sea harvested fields autumn mountains	white mountains ice icicle
HUMANITY	soap bubbles swing sowing seeds	sunglasses hammock barefoot	scarecrow harvest World Series	quilt fireplace ski
OBSERVANCES	Valentine's Day April Fool's Day Easter	summer vacation Mother's Day July 4th	Halloween Rosh Hashanah Basho's birthday	Thanksgiving Christmas Groundhog Day
ANIMALS	butterfly tadpole/frog robin	firefly turtle rainbow trout	dragonfly deer squirrel	winterfly fox owl
PLANTS	apple blossoms dandelion willow	sunflower corn tassles cherries	acorn maple leaves apple	withered rose fallen leaves bare tree

Tool Three: Chart of Shisan Form

Remember, the shisan requires three links in four sections, for a total of twelve links. Here's a sample of a basic shisan chart:

Here are suggestions for charts for shisan renku. Note that there are many possibilities, but there must always be at least one no-season verse between verses with different seasons. Also, seasons flow in their natural order.

SHISAN CHART FOR SPRING

LINK#	SEASON	SPECIAL TOPIC
1. [3 lines] [hokku] greeting; tell place presents season/nature image	spring	blossom ❁
2. [2 lines] [wakiku] link to link #1	spring	
3. [3 lines] [daisan] leap to new topic	no season	
4. [2 lines] link to #3	no season	
5. [3 lines] link to #4	summer	love ❤
6. [2 lines] link to #5	no season	love ❤
7. [3 lines] link to #6	no season	
8. [2 lines] link to #7	autumn	
9. [3 lines] link to #8	autumn	moon ☽
10. [2 lines] link to #9	no season	
11. [3 lines] link to #10	winter	
12. [2 lines] upbeat; closing	no season	

SHISAN CHART FOR THE FOUR SEASONS

no season = ns

starting season	SPRING =sp	SUMMER =su	AUTUMN =au	WINTER =wi
link #				
1	sp/blossom	su	au/moon	wi/blossom
2	sp	su	au	wi
3	ns	ns	ns	ns
4	ns	ns/love	ns	sp
5	su/love	au/moon/love	wi	sp/moon
6	ns/love	au	ns	ns
7	ns	ns	sp/blossom	ns/love
8	au	wi	sp	su/love
9	au/moon	ns	ns	ns
10	ns	ns	ns/love	ns
11	ns	sp/blossom	su/love	au
12	wi	sp	ns	au

KIDS' SHISAN (EXAMPLE FOR SPRING)

"Valentine Chocolate"

(Shisan renku, led by Kris Kondo, Biblioteka Library, Tokyo, Japan, February 15, 2003)

n=Nozomi Onozawa, age ten   h=Helen Ikawa, age ten   m=Masako Kamoto, age ten

LINK	SEASON	SPECIAL TOPIC	LINK	SEASON	SPECIAL TOPIC
1. his mother bows after I hand her, her son's Valentine chocolate n	spring	love	7. curly-headed mustache under his sharp nose the old carpenter h	no season	
2. is it a butterfly or flower on the yellow hat? h	spring	flower	8. moonlight on hamsters' graves zombies arise from the dirt m	autumn	moon
3. laughing and laughing as we unscramble an e-mail Chinese and Japanese m	no season		9. a scary scarecrow a place to gather for noisy birds h	autumn	
4. not waiting for Dad, but for souvenirs from far away n	no season		10. the mystery solved who opened the barn door m	no season	
5. a thousand books my ships, trains, planes, and rockets for summer vacation m	summer		11. for Christmas dolls in kimonos sent over mountains and seas n	winter	
6. a beaded wooden box for our shell collection n	no season		12. setting out and lighting candles along the sidewalk h	no season	

Shisan Warm-Up Exercises

Now that you have been introduced to renku, you're ready to write your own. Here are some exercises to get you started.

Word Association Game

One person says a season word like *summer*, and then the next person says a word connected to summer, like *beach*. And the next person connects to the word *beach* with a word like *waves* . . . and the next person connects to the word *waves* and by saying *radio*, and so on. After going around the circle a few times, another person chooses a new season word. This is a helpful and fun practice—try it!

Link and Shift: Three-Link Practice (for Three People)

This is a chance to write just one link each with a group of three people. The first three links are the hardest of a renku, so it is good to practice them.

Link one (*hokku*): a greeting, often about the place; use the present season (spring, summer, autumn, or winter) or weather of the day
Link two: (*wakiku*): link to link one; follow the chart for the season
Link three (*daisan*): shift or leap to another topic; follow the chart for the season

Here is a kids' example of the three-link practice:

one more birthday gift _____
the blossoms scatter _____
as we play hide and seek _____

—Karen Kondo (age ten, Japan)

a rope of frog eggs _____
getting longer and longer _____

—Masako Kamoto (age ten, Japan)

after it is cut _____
looking in the mirror _____
wanting my hair back _____

—Helen Ikawa (age ten, Japan)

Writing a Shisan (for a Small Group of Two to Six People)

The shisan is a challenge to write. After you have read about the pointers and tools for renku, and have tried the warm-up exercises, you are ready to try the shisan renku form. First you make a za, a circle of friends, and then you can begin your linked verse of twelve links. Use the shisan chart and sample on pages 52–53 as a model to follow. See the chart for the season you are in today and follow it closely. Then pick one person in your group to begin the renku. The *hokku* (first link of three lines) is important, as it sets the mood—it should tell the season and the place. The next link of two lines links directly to the first link. And then the third link of three lines leaps into a new direction. The rest of the links keep linking to the one before it. Check the chart to see what season or special topic word is needed for each link. Just keep your imagination running and enjoy the harmony of the group poem you create. If you keep practicing, you can do it. However, if you want to try some easier forms, try the following.

Writing in Easier Renga Linking Forms

Tan-renga (With a Partner)

Tan-renga is a linked tanka poem (the five-line form) done with a partner. The first person writes three lines (of five-seven-five syllables) about something with nature images, and then the other person writes two lines (of seven-seven syllables) about his or her feeling. For example:

Person A

_____on this moonlit night
_____the crickets sing
_____so loudly

Person B

_____I remember that time
_____listening with you

Rengay (For Two or Three People)

This is new free-form renga created by American haiku poet Garry Gay. *Rengay* links tanka-like lines, but it has no set rules like renku—there is no worry about linking and shifting, a topic checklist, saijiki, or charts to follow. Rengay is a linked verse around a theme (which does not always have to be about nature) like "The Milky Way" or "A Train Trip"—it is *not* a story, but each link does connect to the subject. Rengay can be done by two or three people, and it has six links (3 lines, 2 lines, 3 lines, 3 lines, 2 lines, 3 lines). The only rule is not to repeat any words (nouns or verbs); of course, little words like a, an, the, in, on, over, and so on, are okay. This is an easy and enjoyable linking poem. Here is a rengay sample:

Serenade

harvesting pears
from my backyard
I feel wealthy

glowing gold
the sun hands in the branches

turning from its bowl
the cat licks its paws and yawns—
cool evening breeze

the potter's wheel
turns slowly under old leaves—
shadows changing shapes

a game of catch
extends into moonlight

back and forth
a slow exchange
between crickets

—John Thompson and Garry Gay (from *Frogpond* magazine, 1998, xxi:1)

Gunsaku

This form links haiku with a theme seen from different angles, like "The World Viewed by a Cat." Each haiku can stand alone, and is usually done by one person, but could be done with friends, in which each person adds the three lines of his or her haiku. Try linking six to twelve haiku, but do as few or as many as you like. Try one hundred! Then you can also add drawings to it and make a little book.

Rensaku

This form links haiku with a theme, but this form is like a story, like "The Death of My Cat." Yet, each haiku could stand alone, even though it is part of a bigger story. They are usually done alone, but could be done with friends. Do six to twelve or

however many you like. Illustrate the linked haiku story with drawings, like making a series of haiga (haiku and drawings). This would also make a great mini-book (see page 57).

■   ■   ■

There is no other poetry quite like this in the world. Japan has always had in its culture this unique social poetry. Because renga is group poetry, it is very different from solo haiku, and so its purpose is somewhat different, too. Haiku's main point is to connect to nature; renga's main point is to connect to both people *and* nature. Writing renga helps us to learn cooperation with others. When we do a group poem together, we share an experience. When we share our experience of nature and of our whole world, we are able to touch other people through our words. So, we are linking more than poems, we are linking people, and we are linking our worlds. This brings understanding between people. If more people did renga it could bring more peace to the world. And since haiku long ago came out of the renga tradition, doing renga is like sharing a haiku experience.

1. Making a Small Book

(Designed by Daniel Donegan)

You can make a small book in which to write your haiku and make drawings. You can even use it for group renku, or for haiga, haibun, and series of poems, too. Here are directions on how to make a small book with one sheet of folded paper:

■ Take one sheet of blank paper of any size, but 8 ¹/₂" x 14" (21 ¹/₂ x 35 ¹/₂ cm) is best.

■ Fold the paper lengthwise, like this:

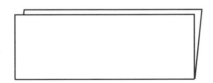

■ Next, fold the paper into four sections, like this:

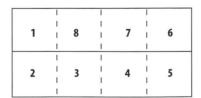

making a small book and other haiku activities

■ Now fold the paper in half again. Cut with scissors between 3 and 8 like this:

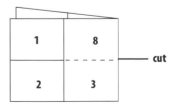

■ Unfold the paper and then fold it in half again vertically. The cut will be in the middle on the top. It will look like this:

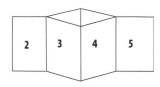

■ Then fold into a little book by pushing section 5 between the cut pages, like this:

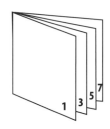

front page: # 1	second page: # 5 and #6
inside cover: # 2	inside back cover: # 7
first page: # 3 and # 4	back page: # 8

You can write the title, your name, and the date on the front page, and inside put one to three haiku, renga, or other poems and sketches on each page. Make copies to keep and give away to friends.

2. Calligraphy

With a brush and black ink, write a haiku on a *shikishi* (square cardboard) or *tanzaku* (long strip of cardboard).

3. Cell Phone Haiku and E-mail Linked Verse

You can enjoy using whatever modern technology you have, like the cell phone, to send short word haiku messages to friends and to the world! You can have fun with your friends by doing a chain-linked poem by e-mail. This is especially handy if you live far from each other; it could also be a good way to make other poet friends from other parts of your country or even from other countries.

4. Haiku Greeting Cards and Party Name Cards

Make your own greeting card with a haiku inside. Some card companies are already making haiku cards, but you can make your own personal ones. For a party, write a haiku on each guest's name card at the table. You can also write haiku on paper cups and plates, and even balloons.

5. Haiku Telegram

Write a message shorter than a haiku—a few words making a short message, for example, "peace will bloom." Draw or paint a picture of the earth or a flower to go with the words. Paul Reps's book *Zen*

Inklings is a good example of these "telegrams" which teach the power of just a few words, as in haiku.

6. Ikebana
Make a flower arrangement and add a haiku card to it, inspired by the flowers.

7. Kuhi (Poem Stone)
Carving a poem on a stone is a tradition in countries in East Asia, such as China, Korea, and Japan. These stones, called *kuhi* in Japanese, are often seen in the high mountains or in special gardens, temples, and parks. The haiku by Sato Kazuo (on page 20) is on the second American kuhi; it can be seen in a garden in Hayward, California. The first and only other American kuhi is in a Japanese garden in Seattle, Washington. Make your own kuhi by finding smooth, large rocks and painting your haiku on them in black or colored paint; however, sometimes you might need permission to do this.

8. Picture-Haiku Album
Cut out photos of nature from magazines, paste them into a notebook, and add a haiku to each picture, either your haiku or another's. This can be done by yourself or with friends in a group.

9. Tanzaku
This long strip of heavy paper to write a haiku on is hung on bamboo trees for festivals, especially on *Tanabata,* the star festival held every July 7 in Japan.

You could also hang these tanzaku in the house, or anywhere—make it a surprise for someone to find. If heavy white cardboard is used, the tanzaku could be put in a frame or holder and placed on the wall as art decoration, as in Japan.

10. Weathergram
Write a haiku on a long strip of heavy paper approximately 6–10" long and 2–3" wide (15–25 x 6–8 cm) and then attach a string to it and hang it outside on a tree branch, letting the wind carry the haiku greeting to others. Let the writing hang in all kinds of weather—sunny, rainy, snowy, windy—until it, too, is blown away. This strip of paper can also be hung from a string to a bell clapper, as done in Japan.

Glossary of Haiku-Related Words

ginko: a walk outside to observe nature and write haiku

gunsaku: a series of haiku done on one subject or theme from different angles, for example, "Views of a Cat"; each haiku can stand alone; is usually done by one person, but could be done by several

haibun: a mini story or prose in sentences or paragraphs, with a haiku added, usually at the end or mixed in

haiga: a haiku with an illustration or painting

haiku: a short (one breath long) Japanese poem with a seventeen-syllable count (of five-seven-five syllables) or three lines in English, usually about nature and centered on one moment; the word *haiku* is used for one poem or many poems (the plural form does not take an *s* at the end)

hokku: the beginning three lines of a renga/renku (linked poem); later in the late nineteenth century, this itself became known as haiku

image: a description or picture in words that appeals to the senses of seeing, hearing, smelling, tasting, and touching; for example: a white cat lying in the green grass

kigo: a season word referring to the details within the season; for example, for the winter season, a kigo might be *icicle, Christmas*, or *freezing wind;* often haiku in English just use a nature image or nature word without telling the exact season (as a kigo would), words such as *rain* or *forest* would be examples.

kireji: A cutting word. A break or pause in a haiku, usually after the first or second line, that makes a contrast or spark between two parts of the haiku images; in Japanese, cutting words like *ya, keri, kana* are used to emphasize the feeling; in English, this is done with punctuation like a dash, comma, colon, or exclamation point

nature image: a word or words referring to nature, which might or might not tell the exact season, such as river, a deep mountain forest, birds in an oak tree—these images are about nature but could be in any season; most haiku in English use as least a nature word or image (if not a kigo) to make good haiku

renga: a linked verse of usually thirty-six or one hundred links, with each link having two or three lines done by a group of people; became popular in Japan in the fourteenth century and is still written today; also an American umbrella term often used for all linked verse

rengay: modern form of linked verse using a theme (which does not always have to be about nature) like "mountains" or "cars," using six links (of three lines and two lines), done by two or three people

renku: the modern word used for the old haikai no renga (linked verse); when Basho's style of linked verse is written today it is called renku

rensaku: a series of haiku done on one subject or theme to make a story; yet the haiku still could stand alone, or go together in a sequence; for example, "The Death of My Cat"; usually done by one person, but could be done by several

senryu: a cousin of haiku; a humorous haiku usually about people rather than nature; like haiku, it came out of the renga (linked verse) form; sometimes it is hard to tell the difference between humorous haiku and senryu

shasei: "a sketch" from nature, when writing a haiku; a word made by haiku poet Shiki

shisan: one kind of renku, a chain poem of twelve links, done by several people

tanka: before the birth of haiku, the court poetry of five lines (a five-seven-five-seven-seven- or thirty-one syllable count in Japanese); this form was later used for the linked verse

tan-renga: a linked tanka poem, done between two people, having two parts, three lines and two lines, making five lines (in a five-seven-five-seven-seven syllable count in Japanese)

waka: an overall word used for "Japanese poetry"; from the eighth century, the traditional court poetry of thirty one syllables of five phrases (five-seven-five-seven-seven); later used in the renga, if written in modern times, a *tanka*

Haiku Resource Guide

Here is a listing of useful resources to further your enjoyment in haiku.

Web Sites
www.jal-foundation.or.jp/html/haiku
www.haiku.com
www.haikuhut.com
www.haiku.insouthsea.co.uk
www.haikuworld.org
www.haikuworldclub.org
www.renku.net
www.tecnet.or.jp/haiku

Resource Centers
The Museum of Haiku Literature:
   www.2.famille.ne.jp/-haiku/index-e-html
American Haiku Archives:
   www.adianta.com/archives

Haiku Groups or Clubs
Haiku Society of America: www.has-haiku.org
Yuki Teikei Haiku Society: www.youngleaves.org

Haiku Magazines
Frogpond: www.octet.com/˜hsa/
The Heron's Nest: www.theheronsnest.com
Mayfly: www.Family-net.net/˜brooksbooks
Modern Haiku: www.modernhaiku.org

Haiku Contests
JAL Foundation
JAL Building
2-4-11 Higashi-Shinagawa
Shinagawa-ku
Tokyo 140-002, Japan
www.jal-foundation.or.jp/html/haiku/english/EL-HaikuContest.htm
The "JAL World Children's Haiku Contest" is the largest contest held once every two years; it publishes the best haiku in an anthology and gives prizes. Winners also attend "a world children's haiku camp" in Japan to learn about Japanese culture.

Haiku Society of America
www.has-haiku.org/res-hsa-contests.htm
The largest and most established haiku contest is its "Nicholas Virgilio Contest" for high school students (grades 7–12). Information on this, and other HSA contests for adults is on their web site.

Modern Haiku
www.modernhaiku.org/issue33-3/awards33-3.html
Their "High School Haiku Scholarship" is a contest for younger poets. See web site for complete information.

The Haiku World Club
www.haikuworldclub.org
British-American site with James Hackett and Susumu Takiguchi; important and biggest world haiku network for haiku poets with good resource information. This site of many links has a long listing of all the on-going major haiku contests.

Bibliography

Behn, Harry, trans. *Cricket Songs: Japanese Haiku*. New York: Harcourt, Brace & World, Inc., 1964.

Blyth, R. H. *Haiku,* vol. 1. 2. 3. 4. Tokyo: Hokuseido Press, 1949–1952.

———. *A History of Haiku*, vols. 1, 2. Tokyo: Hokuseido Press, 1963–64.

Bowers, Faubion, ed., *An Anthology of Classic Haiku: From Sogi to Shiki*. New York: Dover Publications, Inc., 1997.

Coronet Films. *Haiku: An Introduction to Poetry*.

Donegan, Patricia, and Yoshie Ishibashi. *Chiyo-ni: Woman Haiku Master*. Tokyo: Tuttle Publishing, 1998.

Findly, Seaton, ed., and Bob Cooper. *Haiku: Short Poetry of Japan (a film)*. Tokyo: International Motion Picture Co., Inc.

Ginsberg, Allen. *Mostly Sitting Haiku*. Paterson, NJ: From Here Press, 1978.

Giroux, Joan. *The Haiku Form*. Tokyo. Charles E. Tuttle Company, 1974.

Hamill, Sam. *The Sound of Water: Haiku by Basho, Buson, Issa, and Other Poets*. Boston and London: Shambhala, 1995.

———. *Matsuo Basho's The Narrow Road to the Interior*. Boston and London: Shambhala, 1991.

Henderson, Harold. *Haiku in English*. Tokyo: Charles E. Tuttle Company, 1974.

———. *An Introduction to Haiku: An Anthology of Poems and Poets from Basho to Shiki*. New York: Anchor Books, 1958.

Higginson, William J. *The Haiku Seasons: Poetry of the Natural World*. Tokyo: Kodansha International, 1996.

———. *An International Poetry Almanac*. Tokyo: Kodansha International, 1997.

Higginson, William J., with Penny Harter. *The Haiku Handbook: How to Write, Share, and Teach Haiku*. New York: McGraw-Hill, 1985.

Higginson, William J., and Tadashi Kondo. *Link and Shift: A Practical Guide to Renku Composition*. Tokyo Seikei University, 1994.

Kato, Koko, and David Burleigh, trans. *A Hidden Pond: Anthology of Modern [Japanese] Haiku*. Tokyo: Kadokawa Shoten, 1997.

Kerouac, Jack. *Scattered Poems*. San Francisco: City Lights Books, 1970.

Mayhew, Lenore. *Monkey's Raincoat: Linked Poetry of the Basho School with Haiku Selections*. Tokyo: Charles E. Tuttle Company, 1985.

Miura, Yuzuru. *Classic Haiku: A Master's Selection*. Tokyo: Charles E. Tuttle Company, 1991.

Oseko, Toshihara. *Basho's Haiku: Literal Translations for Those Who Wish to Read the Original Japanese Text, with Grammatical Analysis and Explanatory Notes*. Tokyo: Maruzen Co., Ltd., 1990.

Reps, Paul. *Gold and Fish Signatures*. Rutland, VT: Charles E. Tuttle Co., 1968.

Ross, Bruce. *Haiku Moment: An Anthology of Contemporary North American Haiku*. Rutland, VT: Charles E. Tuttle Company, Inc., 1993.

duck flowing mountain puppy salmon
autumn drizzle marshmallows kitchen
snowflakes kitten food wooden moon
petals geese happy dogs pumpkins evening
baseball calm puppy trees happy doll
skirt branch bamboos sneaker flowers
frog pond water happy pumpkins starlight
grandfather puppy bamboos pumpkin
sailboat branch frog oceanside dewdrops
homework water skirt sailboat dogs rain
dancing trees mountain laughter mom
dogs flowing autumn duck salmon puppy
autumn drizzle marshmallows kitchen rose
snowflakes kitten food wooden on lights
flowers geese happy rain pumpkins